W9-CKB-409

A CATHOLIC CHILD'S
First Prayer Book

Edited by

Rev. Victor Hoagland, C.P.

Illustrated by

Kathy Fincher

Regina Press

The Regina Press
10 Hub Drive
Melville, New York 11747
www.reginapress.com

Copyright © 2007 by the Regina Press. All rights reserved.
Artwork copyright Kathy Fincher © 2007.
No part of this book may be reproduced in any form without
expressed permission from the publisher.

Printed in China.

ISBN 9780882711485

Prayers and Devotions

The Sign of the Cross

In the name of the Father
and of the Son
and of the Holy Spirit. Amen.

Glory Be

Glory be to the Father,
and to the Son,
and to the Holy Spirit,
as it was in the beginning,
is now, and ever shall be,
world without end. Amen.

Grace Before Meals

Bless us, O Lord,
and these Your gifts,
which we are about to receive
from Your bounty,
Through Christ, our Lord. Amen.

Grace After Meals

We give You thanks;
O almighty God,
for all Your benefits;
You who live and reign,
world without end. Amen.

The Lord's Prayer

Our Father, who art in heaven,
hallowed be Thy name;
Thy kingdom come;
Thy will be done on earth
as it is in heaven.
Give us this day our daily bread;
and forgive us our trespasses
as we forgive those who trespass against us
and lead us not into temptation,
but deliver us from evil. Amen.

The Hail Mary

Hail Mary, full of grace.
The Lord is with you.
Blessed are you among women,
and blessed is the fruit,
of your womb, Jesus.
Holy Mary, Mother of God,
pray for us sinners,
now and at the hour
of our death. Amen.

Guardian Angel Prayer

Angel of God
my Guardian dear
to whom God's love
commits me here.
Ever this day
be at my side
to light and guard
to rule and guide.

The Apostles' Creed

I believe in God, the Father almighty,
Creator of heaven and earth.
I believe in Jesus Christ,
his only Son, our Lord.
He was conceived by the power of the
Holy Spirit and born of the Virgin Mary.
He suffered under Pontius Pilate,
was crucified, died and was buried.
He descended to the dead.
On the third day he rose again.
He ascended into heaven,
and is seated at the right hand
of the Father.
He will come again to judge
the living and the dead.
I believe in the Holy Spirit,
the holy catholic Church,
the communion of saints,
the forgiveness of sins,
the resurrection of the body,
and life everlasting. Amen.

The 23rd Psalm

The Lord is my Shepherd;
I shall not want.
In verdant pastures He gives me repose;
Before restful waters He leads me;
He refreshes my soul.
He guides me in right paths
for His name's sake.
Even though I walk in the dark
valley I fear no evil;
for you are at my side,
with your rod and your staff
that give me courage.
You spread a table for me
in the sight of my foes;
you anoint my head with oil;
my cup overflows.
Only goodness and kindness follow me all
the days of my life;
And I shall dwell in the house
of the Lord for years to come.

Lord, Make Me An Instrument of Your Peace

Lord, make me an instrument
 of your peace.
Where there is hatred, let me sow love;
Where there is injury, pardon;
Where there is discord, let me sow union;
Where there is doubt, faith;
Where there is despair, hope;
Where there is darkness, light;
And where there is sadness, joy;
Grant that I may not so much seek
to be consoled, as to console;
To be understood, as to understand;
To be loved, as to love;
For it is in giving that we receive.
It is in pardoning that we are pardoned;
And it is in dying,
that we are born to eternal life.

St. Francis of Assisi

The Sacraments

Baptism

Confirmation

Holy Eucharist

Reconciliation

Anointing of the Sick

Holy Orders

Matrimony

The Beatitudes

Blessed are the poor in spirit, for the kingdom of heaven is theirs.

Blessed are those who are sad, for they shall be comforted.

Blessed are the mild and gentle, for they shall inherit the land.

Blessed are those who hunger and thirst for justice, for they shall be filled.

Blessed are the merciful, for they shall receive mercy.

Blessed are the pure in heart, for they shall see God.

Blessed are those who make peace, for they shall be called the peacemakers.

Blessed are those who suffer for My sake, for heaven will be theirs.

The Chief Corporal Works of Mercy

To feed the hungry.

To give drink to the thirsty.

To clothe the naked.

To visit the imprisoned.

To shelter the homeless.

To visit the sick.

To bury the dead.

The Chief Spiritual Works of Mercy

To admonish the sinner.

To instruct the ignorant.

To counsel the doubtful.

To comfort the sorrowful.

To bear wrongs patiently.

To forgive all injuries.

To pray for the living and the dead.

The Ten Commandments

I, the Lord, am your God. You shall not have other gods besides me.

You shall not take the name of the Lord, your God, in vain.

Remember to keep holy the sabbath day.

Honor your father and your mother.

You shall not kill.

You shall not commit adultery.

You shall not steal.

You shall not bear false witness against your neighbor.

You shall not covet your neighbor's wife.

You shall not covet anything that belongs to your neighbor.

The Rosary

The Joyful Mysteries
The Annunciation
The Visitation
The Birth of Jesus
The Presentation of Jesus in the Temple
The Finding of Jesus in the Temple

The Luminous Mysteries
The Baptism of Jesus
The Wedding at Cana
The Proclamation of the Kingdom of God
The Transfiguration
The Institution of the Holy Eucharist

The Sorrowful Mysteries
The Agony in the Garden
The Scourging of Jesus
The Crowning of Jesus with Thorns
The Carrying of the Cross
The Death of Jesus on the Cross

The Glorious Mysteries
The Resurrection
The Ascension
The Coming of the Holy Spirit
The Assumption of Mary
The Coronation of Mary in Heaven

Personal Record

Name _____

    Born _____ in _____

Baptism

    Date _____

    Priest _____

    Parish _____

    Godfather _____

    Godmother _____

First Communion

    Date _____

    Priest _____

    Parish _____

Confirmation

    Date _____

    Bishop _____

    Parish _____

    Sponsor _____

    Confirmation Name _____

Family Record

Father _____

    Born _____ in _____

Mother _____

    Born _____ in _____

Brothers and Sisters _____

_____

_____

Father's Family

    Grandfather _____

       Born _____

    Grandmother _____

       Born _____

Mother's Family

    Grandfather _____

       Born _____

    Grandmother _____

       Born _____

This is my own prayer
thanking God for my friends...

This is my own prayer thanking God for my family...

This is my own prayer
thanking God for the day...

_____

_____

_____

_____

_____

_____

_____

_____

_____

_____

_____

_____

_____

_____

This is my bed time prayer...